World Book, Inc.
180 North LaSalle Street
Suite 900
Chicago, Illinois 60601
USA

For information about other "True or False?" titles, as well as other World Book print and digital publications, please go to www.worldbook.com.

For information about other World Book publications, call 1-800-WORLDBK (967-5325).

For information about sales to schools and libraries, call 1-800-975-3250 (United States) or 1-800-837-5365 (Canada).

Library of Congress Cataloging-in-Publication Data for this volume has been applied for.

True or False?
ISBN: 978-0-7166-4069-1 (set, hc.)

Incredible Kids
ISBN: 978-0-7166-4074-5 (hc.)

Also available as:
ISBN: 978-0-7166-4084-4 (e-book)

Printed in the United States of America by CG Book Printers, North Mankato, Minnesota

1st printing March 2020

Staff

Executive Committee

President
Geoff Broderick

Vice President, Finance
Donald D. Keller

Vice President, Marketing
Jean Lin

Vice President, International
Maksim Rutenberg

Vice President, Technology
Jason Dole

Director, Content and Product Development
Tom Evans

Director, Human Resources
Bev Ecker

Editorial

Writer
Madeline King

Manager, New Content Development
Jeff De La Rosa

Librarian
S. Thomas Richardson

Manager, Indexing Services
David Pofelski

Digital

Director, Digital Product Development
Erika Meller

Digital Product Manager
Jonathan Wills

Graphics and Design

Senior Designers
Don Di Sante
Isaiah Sheppard

Senior Visual Communications Designer
Melanie Bender

Media Editor
Rosalia Bledsoe

Manufacturing/Production

Manufacturing Manager
Anne Fritzinger

Production Specialist
Curley Hunter

Proofreader
Nathalie Strassheim

TRUE OR FALSE?

INCREDIBLE KIDS

WORLD BOOK

www.worldbook.com

You have to be at least 16 years old
to be incredible.

People of all ages can be
incredible. What incredible
things will you do?

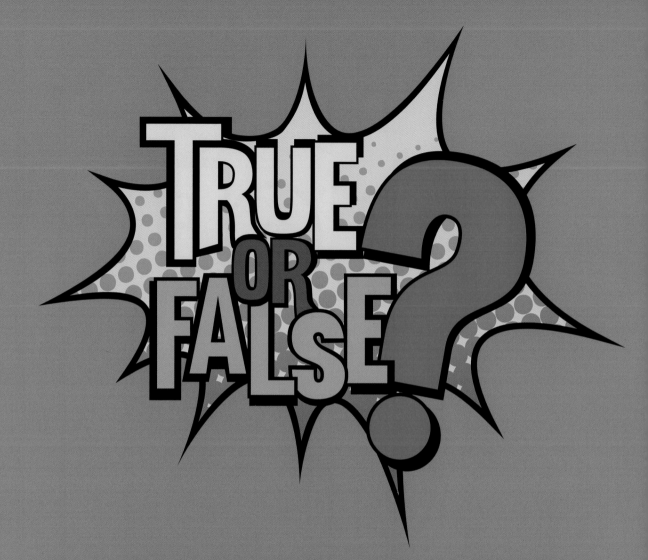

TRUE OR FALSE?

A teenager invented *braille,* a system of reading used by people with blindness and other vision problems.

At the age of 15, the Frenchman Louis
Braille (1809-1852) developed the writing
system that bears his name. He had been
blinded in an accident at age three. Braille
is written in raised dots and read by touch.

a b c d e f g

h i j k l m n

o p q r s t u

v w x y z

In 1960, six-year-old Ruby Bridges was arrested for protesting *segregation* (separation based on race).

PUBLIC SCHOOL

Ruby Bridges was one of the first black students to integrate an elementary school in the Deep South region of the United States. (Before that time, blacks in the Deep South were not allowed in white schools.) Ruby bravely walked pass protesters to her class.

TRUE OR FALSE?

Kids have invented such fun things as toy trucks, trampolines, and popsicles.

TRUE!

Kids invented these fun things and many others. You might enjoy playing with toy trucks. But don't try to double your fun by jumping on a trampoline *with* a popsicle.

TRUE OR FALSE?

Albert Einstein named the dwarf planet Pluto.

Pluto

In 1930, an 11-year-old girl in England suggested the name for the newly discovered object. Her name was Venetia Burney.

Easton LaChappelle was the youngest architect in history. His first masterpiece was a *chapel,* a building for religious worship.

False! LaChappelle is an American engineer. As a teenager, he created a robotic hand and, eventually, an entire robotic arm.

26

The American athlete Simone Biles
became the first gymnast in Olympic
history to earn a perfect score.

AMF

The Romanian gymnast Nadia Coma-
neci was the first to get a perfect
score. In 1976, at the age of 14, she
scored a perfect 10.0 for her skills
on the uneven bars.

TRUE OR FALSE?

[A]nne Frank, a German
[Jewis]h girl, wrote a diary while
[hidin]g from the Nazis during
[Wo]rld War II (1939-1945).

en grappen. Dan hoe de lessen zijn.
2e deel. Anne met Wikke en op school.
In het kamertje met Kitty en haar jongens
waaronder Kermd aan theetafel bezig
dan op school ongeluk door een storm
hun kinderen en allerlei diverse tonelen
b.v. in bed met Peter en aan tafel.
3e deel. Anne haar toiletten de P.Maria
... juichen opjerk die cadeau van Wikke
Wikke en schoenen.

16 Oct. 1942

Anne Frank

Lieve Marianne, 10 Oct. 1942 Zondag
gisteren is het
schrijven er weer bij
ingeschoten. Teneerste
omdat ik de lijst van
Franse werkwoorden wilde
afmaken en ben tweede
omdat ik ook nog ander
werk had. Ik heb weer
4 boeken van kleiman ge-
kregen, De Arcadia. Dat han-
delt over een reis naar Spits-

bergen en De Louteringskuur, zo lijken me wel leuk.
De Opstandelingen heeft ze ook mee gebracht. Dat
is van Ammers küller. Dezelfde schrijfster als van
Heeren, Vrouwen, Knechten. Dit mag ik nu ook lezen
Dan heb ik een heleboel liefde's roman toneelschri...
van körner gelezen, ik vind dat die man leukeschr...
B.v. Hedwig, der
Vetter aus Brehem,
Hans Heilings Felsen,
Der Grüne, Domino,
Die Gouvernante,
Der Vierjährige
Posten, Die Sühne,
Der Kamf mit dem
Drachen, Der Nacht-
Wächter en zoal
meer. Vader wil dat
ik nu ook Hebbel en
andere boeken van
andere welbekende
Duitse schrijvers
ga lezen. Het Duits
lezen, gaat nu al be-
trekkelijk vlot. Alleen
fluister ik het meestal, inplaats dat ik
mezelf lees. Maar dat gaat wel over. Gisteren

Dit is een
foto, zoals
ik me zou
wensen,
altijd zo
te zijn.
Dan had
ik nog wel een kans
om naar Holywood te
komen. Maar tegen-
woordig zie ik er
jammer genoeg meer
al anders uit.
Annefrank
10 Oct. 19..
Zondag

Frank started writing her diary when she was 13. The diary was published in 1947 and has been translated into more than 60 languages.

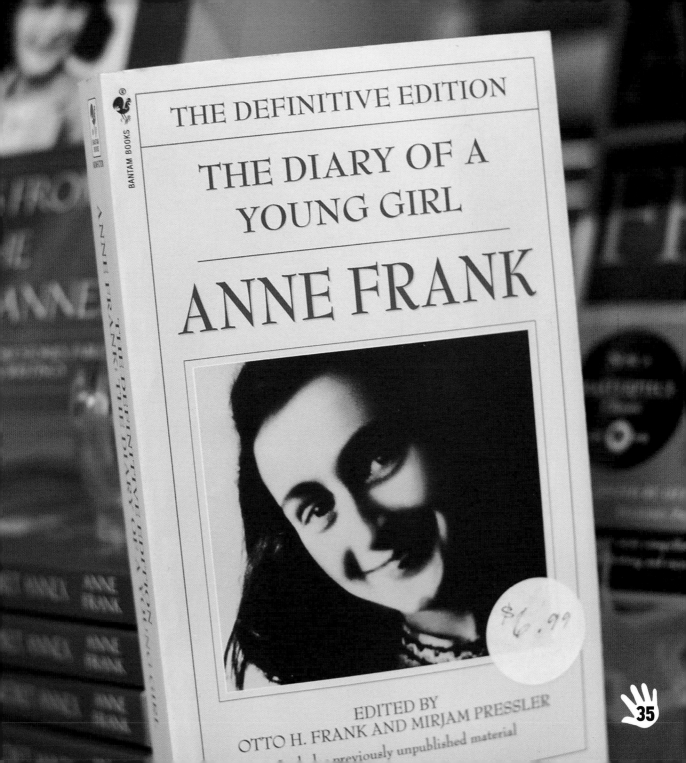

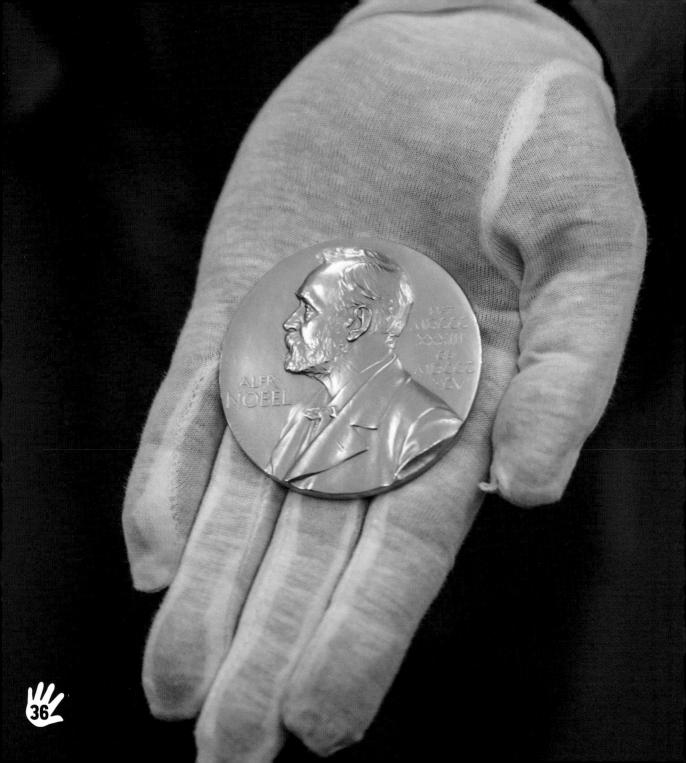

TRUE OR FALSE?

You must be at least 21 to win a *Nobel prize,* an award that honors someone who has made significant contributions to the "good of humanity."

37

Malala Yousafzai won the Nobel Peace Prize when she was 17. Yousafzai survived an attempt on her life by attackers who did not think girls should be allowed to attend school. Now she campaigns for the education of young girls.

38

39

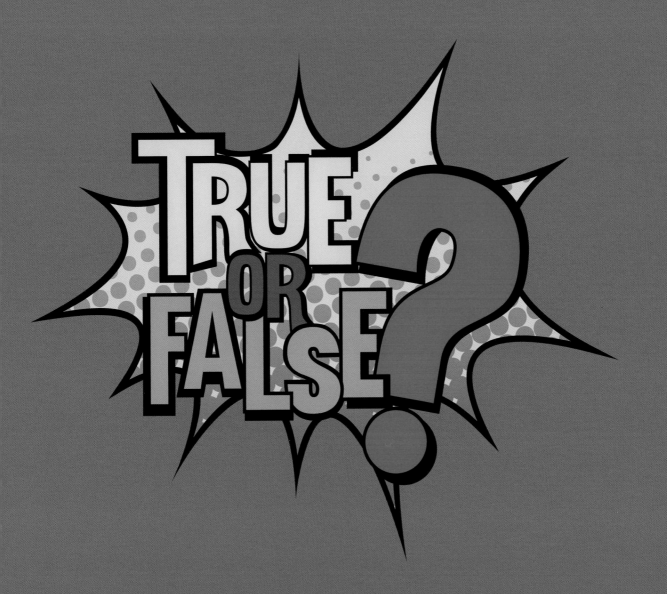

TRUE OR FALSE?

Solving math problems can
be a circus act.

41

A math whiz at age five, Shakuntala Devi (1929-2013) from India began solving difficult math problems at circuses. She was known as "the human computer." When she was older, she correctly multiplied two 13-digit numbers in 28 seconds.

Jazz Jennings is a famous dancer. When she was 11, she became a star of the New York City Ballet.

BOX OFFICE HOURS: 2 HOURS BEFORE
SAT 10 AM - 2 PM

45

Jazz Jennings is an activist for LGBTQ rights. **LGBTQ** is an abbreviation for *l*esbian, *g*ay, *b*isexual, *t*ransgender, and *q*ueer or *q*uestioning. A transgender woman, she became known as a teenage advocate for transgender rights.

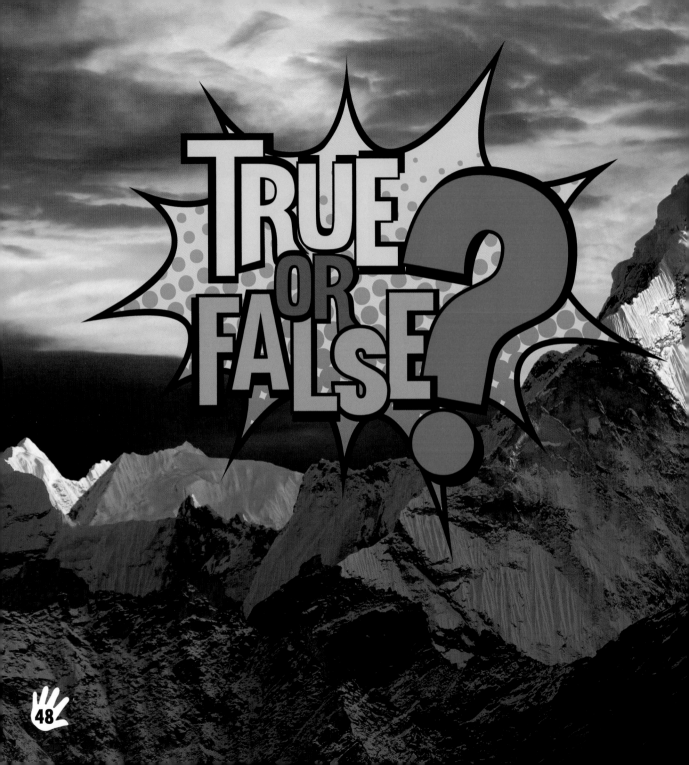

A 13-year-old climbed Mount Everest.

49

Jordan Romero reached the top of the highest mountain in the world in 2010. At the top, he telephoned his mother.

Some kids *really* like school.

Some kids not only like school, they help others *go to school* and stay in school. When Thandiwe Chama of Zambia, in Africa, was eight, her school was forced to close. She encouraged children to march to another school to be admitted.

Joan of Arc created the *croissant*,
a crescent-shaped buttery,
flaky pastry.

57

Joan of Arc (1412?-1431) was a military leader inspired by heavenly voices and visions of the saints. When she was 18, she led the French army to victory against the English.

TRUE OR FALSE?

Hamburger grease can heat
a home.

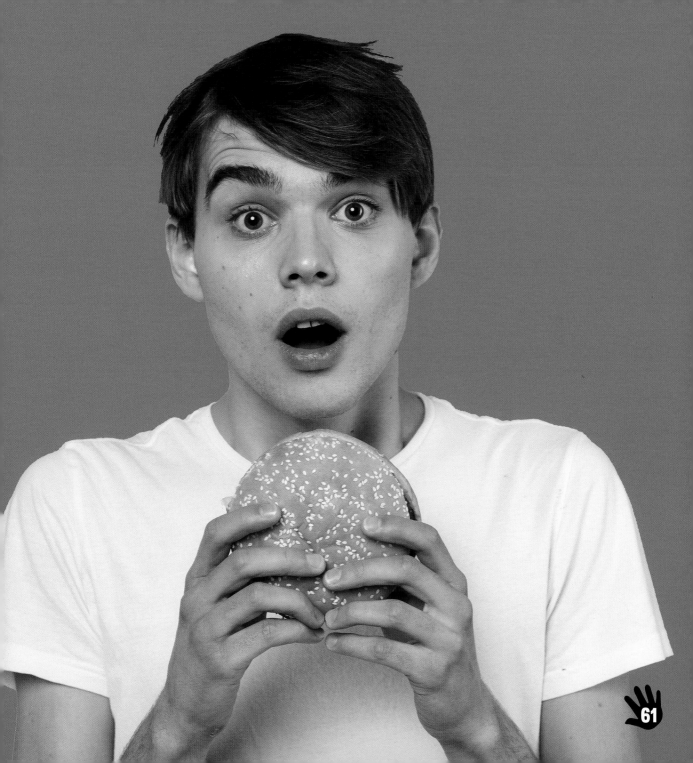

When she was eleven, the American Cassandra Lin founded Turn Grease Into Fuel (TGIF). The organization collects kitchen grease, recycles it, and shares it with people in need.

Cassandra

COOKING

The Austrian composer Wolfgang Amadeus Mozart created his first piece of music at age 13.

Mozart (1756-1791) started composing music at age five. When he was six, he played for the Austrian empress at her court in Vienna.

**Sophie Cruz is a young,
Mexican pop star**

69

Sophie Cruz is an immigration activist. She is the American-born child of Mexican parents. When she was five, Cruz wrote a letter to the pope, the head of the Roman Catholic Church. Her letter translated to, "My friends and I love each other no matter our skin color."

I AM AN IMMIGRANT

TRUE OR FALSE?

Incredible things are always
done by people working alone.

Groups of kids can do incredible things. For instance, they can organize marches that bring attention to important causes.

TRUE OR FALSE?

Seventeen-year-old cellist Sheku Kanneh-Mason became the first black musician to win the British Broadcasting Corporation's Young Musician of the Year Award.

And the following year Kanneh-Mason was invited to play at the wedding of Prince Harry and Meghan Markle, the Duke and Duchess of Sussex, in England.

Missing school can have a positive impact on the world.

TRUE!

But the reason has to be *really, really* good. Greta Thunberg, a Swedish environmental activist, missed many days of school to protest for action on climate change. She inspired other student protesters to do the same.

Kids of all abilities can achieve great things.

When she was three, Najla Imad Lafta of Iraq lost three limbs after a bomb blast. She became a celebrated table tennis player. When she was only 12, she earned a place on Iraq's Paralympic table tennis team.

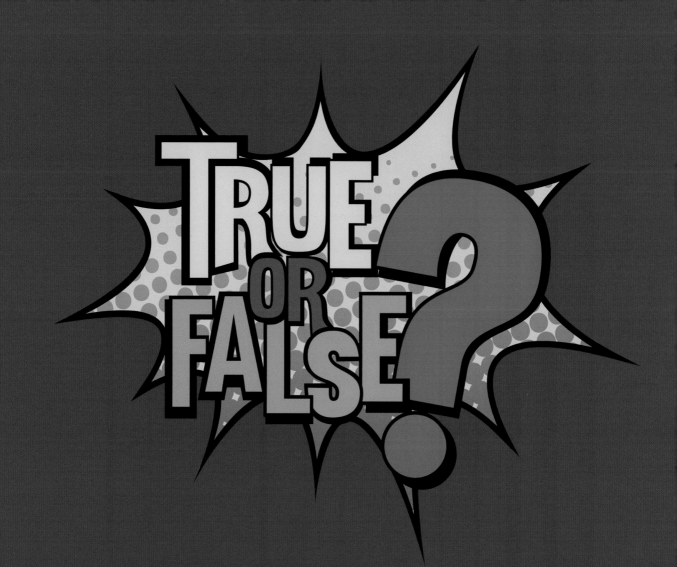

Seven-year-old Bana al-Abed wrote letters to tell the world about her war-torn country of Syria.

With the help of her mother, al-Abed sent messages through Twitter to document the conflict in her home city of Aleppo.

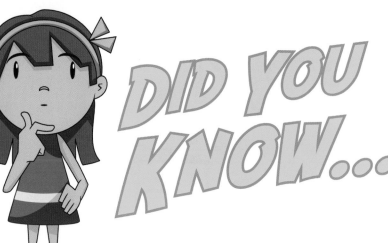

DID YOU KNOW...

The child activist Iqbal Masih (1983-1995) helped over **3,000 children escape slavery** in Pakistan.

Sisters Melati and Isabel Wijsen created an organization called **Bye Bye Plastic Bags.** They work to ban plastic bags as well as clean up the beaches in their home of Bali, an island in Indonesia.

The Greek gymnast Dimitrios Loundras is the **youngest known Olympic medalist.** When he was 10, his team placed third in the parallel bars in the 1896 Olympic Games.

13-year-old scientist Nora Keegan figured out that some hand dryers are loud enough to damage children's ears.

Indigenous and climate activist **Xiuhtezcatl Martinez** began using hip-hop music to spread environmental messages as a teenager.

Index

95

Acknowledgments

Cover: © Africa Studio/Shutterstock; © Sam iSam Miller/Shutterstock; © Helen Field, Shutterstock

5-9	© Shutterstock
11	© James Lee 999/Getty Images
12	© Bettmann/Getty Images
14	© Underwood Archives/Getty Images
16-19	© Shutterstock
21	© Bettmann/Getty Images
22	Public Domain
25	© Morphart Creation/Shutterstock
27	© Microsoft
29	© Pat Scaasi, NurPhoto/Getty Images
30	© Marc Vodofsky, New York Post/ Photo Archives/Getty Images
32-33	© Heritage Images/Getty Images
35	© Andrew Burton, Getty Images
36	© Marc Müller, picture alliance/ Getty Images
39	© Heiko Junge, Getty Images
40-42	© Shutterstock
45	© Alberto E. Rodriguez, Getty Images
46	© Andrew H. Walker, Getty Images
48-49	© Daniel Prudek, Shutterstock
50	© Prakash Mathema, Getty Images
53	© Darrin Henry, Shutterstock
54	© KidsRights
56	© Mindscape studio/Shutterstock
59	Public Domain
61	© ShotPrime Studio/Shutterstock
63	Courtesy of Jason Lin
64-68	© Shutterstock
71	© Vivien Killilea, Getty Images
72-75	© Shutterstock
76	© Richard Martin-Roberts, Getty Images
79	© ROTA/Camera Press/Redux Pictures
80-81	© Alastair Pike, Getty Images
83	© Spencer Platt, Getty Images
85	© Ann Gaysorn, Shutterstock
87	© Ivor Prickett, The New York Times Redux Pictures
89-90	© Thaer Mohammed, Getty Images
92-93	© Shutterstock; © John van Hassel Sygma/Getty Images; © Jörg Carstensen, picture alliance/Getty Images; Public Domain; © Antonio Scorza, Getty Images